SINGULARITY DUAL-ASPECT EMERGENCE

Volume VI

Sacred Divine Spirituality

*From the Ogdoad to Heru: African Cosmology, Mathematics, Ma'at,
and the SDAE Spirit Field*

Aston Farquharson

NuSpecies Press

Pawling, New York

2026

Published by NuSpecies Press, Pawling, New York, USA

nuspecies.com

eBook ISBN: 979-8-9960439-8-9

Paperback ISBN: 979-8-9960439-9-6

Hardcover ISBN: 979-8-9963738-0-2

This book presents Sacred Divine Spirituality and Singularity Dual-Aspect Emergence (SDAE) as philosophical, spiritual, educational, and metaphysical reflection. It does not claim that ancient myth is modern physics, nor that modern physics proves religion. It does not present new physics, new particles, new forces, guarantees of healing, or medical claims.

This book is not a substitute for medical, legal, scientific, theological, psychological, or mental health advice. Readers should work with qualified professionals, including licensed clinicians, for diagnosis, treatment, medical decisions, and personal care.

AI-Assistance Disclosure: This work was created, directed, selected, arranged, revised, and approved by Aston Farquharson. AI-assisted tools were used as editorial, research-organization, drafting-support, formatting, and design-assistance tools. The central concepts, terminology, framework, selection, arrangement, final revisions, and authorial judgment are by Aston Farquharson. Any copyright claim should cover the human-authored material, including original text, revisions, selection, coordination, arrangement, compilation, structure, terminology, and expressive contributions by Aston Farquharson.

Dedication

For NuSpecians, caregivers, seekers, families, healers, scientists, believers, skeptics, the sick, the grieving, the dying, and the living who still want to live in right relationship with body, nature, truth, and the Divine Cosmos.

For the ancestors whose names were translated, renamed, forgotten, or misread, yet whose measure, memory, and Ma'at continue to speak.

Table of Contents

Preface - Why Sacred Divine Spirituality Must Be Rebuilt

There is a form of spirituality that does not ask the human being to flee from nature, distrust the body, or wait for dignity only in another world while neglecting this one. There is a form of spirituality that begins with breath, soil, sunlight, water, stars, ancestry, mathematics, compassion, and the living body. This book calls that form Sacred Divine Spirituality.

Sacred does not mean removed from life. Divine does not mean detached from nature. Spirituality does not mean hostility toward science. In this work, sacred means worthy of reverent care. Divine means participating in the deepest order of reality. Spirituality means coherent resonance between inner and outer life.

Singularity Dual-Aspect Emergence - SDAE - begins from a simple but profound claim: reality is not matter alone, and it is not mind alone. Reality expresses itself through outer structure and inner experience. The physical universe unfolds outward into fields, particles, spacetime, stars, chemistry, biology, and nervous systems. The interior universe unfolds inward into sensation, awareness, emotion, meaning, value, compassion, and coherence.

SDAE calls the structured interior domain of coherence the Spirit Field. Not as a new physical field. Not as a new force. Not as a particle. Not as a substitute for medicine, physics, or religion. The Spirit Field is the name SDAE gives to organized patterns of interior life: meaning, value, ethical resonance, emotional integration, compassion, aesthetic perception, and lived coherence.

This book begins in the symbolic deep of African cosmology, where the ancestors named the world before form. It begins in Khmunu, the City of the Eight. It begins with the Ogdoad. But this is not a book claiming that ancient myth was modern physics. It is not a book claiming that modern physics proves ancient theology. It is a book of disciplined restoration.

The purpose of this book is not to win an argument over the past. The purpose is to help restore a future: a future where science is honored, spirituality becomes responsible, African memory is restored without bitterness, and people who are sick, grieving, aging, and afraid can find dignity in the life they are living now.

The afterlife belongs to each reader's faith tradition. This book concerns the life we must live here: the body we must care for, the Earth we must protect, the relationships we must repair, the coherence we must restore, and the compassion we must not postpone.

NuSpecian sacred form: We come from the cosmos. We are sustained by nature. We become whole through balance. Therefore let body, mind, relation, and Earth be kept in right measure.

Chapter 1 - Why We Return to Kemet and Kush

To return to Kemet and Kush is not to reject the rest of humanity. It is to return to a place where humanity once understood that sky, river, body, mathematics, medicine, morality, architecture, kingship, and spirit belonged to one order of meaning. In the modern world, we divide what the ancestors often held together. We place science in one building, religion in another, medicine in another, ecology in another, philosophy in another, and grief in a private room where people are expected to suffer quietly.

The older Nile Valley imagination did not always divide reality so sharply. The stars were not merely decoration. The river was not merely water. The body was not merely flesh. The heart was not merely an organ. The temple was not merely stone. Measure was not merely arithmetic. Order was not merely law. Nature was not merely background. All were part of a field of relation.

This does not mean every ancient claim was scientifically correct. It does not mean the past should be romanticized. It does not mean every symbol should be converted into a physics equation. It means the ancient world preserved a powerful intuition modern life has nearly forgotten: to live well, the human being must live in right relationship with the whole.

The older names matter because names carry memory. Kemet is not merely "Egypt" as seen through later Greek and European eyes. Kush and Ta-Seti are not footnotes to someone else's civilization. Khmunu is not only Hermopolis. Iunu is not only Heliopolis. Heru is not only Horus. Asar is not only Osiris. Aset is not only Isis. Djehuty is not only Thoth.

The Greek names help modern readers recognize the figures. But the older names help us remember that the story did not begin in translation. This book will therefore speak in two languages at first: the familiar and the restored. Then, as the reader walks deeper into the work, the restored names will take their place. Not to exclude. Not to impress. Not to wage war over syllables. But to practice Ma'at with memory.

There is no need to hate Greece to honor Kemet. There is no need to attack Christianity to study Heru. There is no need to dismiss Judaism or Islam to understand older cosmological patterns of Africa and the ancient Near East. There is no need to reject modern physics to learn from ancient symbolic cosmology.

The higher task is to see how humanity has always reached toward the same great questions: What is the Source? How does order emerge? Why does disorder threaten life? How is coherence restored? What does it mean to live rightly? What remains when the body returns to nature?

SDAE enters this conversation not as final proof, but as a disciplined bridge: one root, two irreducible aspects, outer structure, inner experience, consciousness at the threshold, Spirit as structured interior coherence. The older ancestors might have called right living Ma'at. NuSpecians may call it Sacred Divine Spirituality. The names differ. The demand is the same: live in right relationship.

Chapter 2 - Khmunu and the Ogdoad: The Eightfold Deep

Before the world appears, the human imagination must speak of what is not yet world. It must speak of darkness before sight, depth before surface, hiddenness before revelation, infinity before boundary, and potential before form. The Nile Valley ancestors gave one of these symbolic languages the name of the Ogdoad - the Eight.

In this book, the Ogdoad is not treated as modern physics. It is not offered as evidence for quantum gravity, inflation, or cosmological singularities. It is approached as ancestral symbolic teaching: a way of contemplating primordial potential before differentiated structure.

The Ogdoad gives us four complementary pairs: Nun and Naunet, the deep waters and unformed matrix; Heh and Hauhet, infinity and immeasurable extension; Kek and Kauket, darkness and the unseen condition before light; Amun and Amaunet, hiddenness and the concealed principle not yet manifest. Together they are the symbolic Deep before the world.

In SDAE language, they teach dormant relational potential. Not nothing. Not yet something. Possibility before form. This is where the book must be careful: ancient myth does not become science because we admire it, and modern physics does not become theology because it humbles us. But both can teach reverence.

SDAE Volume II avoids dependence on a literal classical singularity and instead speaks of a primordial undifferentiated condition: a pre-spatial, pre-temporal, pre-geometric philosophical root from which physical structure and experiential interiority may emerge. The Ogdoad becomes an ancestral image for that philosophical boundary.

Before structure, there must be the possibility of structure. Before geometry, there must be relation capable of becoming geometry. Before consciousness, there must be the possibility of interiority. Before mathematics is written, there must be lawful relationship waiting to become intelligible.

In the Ogdoad, mathematics is not yet number. It is not yet geometry. It is not yet equation. It is relation asleep in the Deep. It is pattern before form, law before symbol, coherence before measurement. And as the universe unfolds, mathematics awakens with it: first as symmetry, then as geometry, then as force, then as life, then as mind, and perhaps one day as a deeper language of Spirit, coherence, and perspective still beyond present human imagination.

Chapter 3 - Atum/Ptah and the First Center

Before a universe can unfold, there must be a difference. Before difference, there is no direction. Before direction, there is no path. Before path, there is no geometry. Before geometry, there is no world. The Ogdoad gives us the symbolic Deep, but a deep, however pregnant with possibility, is not yet a world. The Deep must find a center.

In the Heliopolitan tradition of Iunu, that center is Atum, or Re-Atum: the self-arising creator from whom ordered genealogy unfolds. In the Memphite tradition, that creative center is Ptah, the maker and craftsman principle, the one associated with heart and speech. SDAE does not collapse Atum and Ptah into one historical figure. Instead, it reads them as two sacred languages for one philosophical movement: emergence as self-centering, and emergence as articulated ordering.

Atum is the first point. Ptah is the first design. Atum says: reality must gather itself. Ptah says: reality must become expressible. One is the center arising. The other is the center speaking form into intelligibility. In SDAE language, the first center is the symbolic moment when dormant relational potential becomes organized enough to support direction, sequence, distinction, and emergence.

A point has no width, height, or depth. Yet without a point, there is no line. Without a line, no angle. Without an angle, no plane. Without a plane, no boundary. Without boundary, no form. Without form, no world. This is why Atum is so powerful as symbolic mathematics. Atum is the moment when the unmeasured becomes centered.

SDAE may write this symbolically: Omega_8 -> C_1 -> Pi_9. Omega_8 is the eightfold Deep of primordial potential. C_1 is the first center, the emergence point. Pi_9 is the ninefold architecture of differentiated order. This is not physics. It is symbolic ontology. It says the world becomes possible when dormant relation becomes centered relation.

Ptah gives us the next step. The heart holds the form inwardly. Speech projects the form outwardly. In SDAE terms, Ptah is already dual-aspect: inner conception and outer construction, hidden design and spoken order. The world becomes a world when hidden order becomes expressible.

This matters for human life. A person in crisis may be an uncentered Deep: much feeling, memory, pain, fear, hope, and possibility, but no coherent point. Sacred Divine Spirituality asks: where is your center? Not your performance, wound, or public identity. Your center. One breath. One truth. One glass of water. One decision not to become cruel. First gather; then speak form.

Chapter 4 - Iunu and the Pesedjet: The Ninefold Emergence

The Center does not remain alone. Once the Deep finds a center, relation begins. Once relation begins, difference becomes possible. Once difference becomes possible, the world can unfold. In Iunu, later called Heliopolis, the Pesedjet - the Nine, or Ennead - teaches differentiated emergence.

The Pesedjet is not merely a list of deities. It is a symbolic architecture. It teaches that creation is not simply an explosion into things. Creation is the unfolding of relationship: first center, then polarity, separation, boundary, life, disruption, repair, and the need for Ma'at.

From Atum comes Shu and Tefnut. In sacred teaching language, Shu is separation, breath, spacing, atmosphere, and the room life needs to exist. Tefnut is moisture, binding, relational continuity, and the life-bearing condition that prevents space from becoming sterile emptiness. Together they teach that emergence is never only expansion. It is also relation.

Too much separation, and nothing holds. Too much binding, and nothing differentiates. Creation requires both: space and connection, distance and continuity, air and moisture, freedom and relation. A family needs closeness, but also boundaries. A mind needs feeling, but also space. A body needs hydration, but also breath. A civilization needs connection, but also freedom.

From Shu and Tefnut come Geb and Nut: earth and sky. Geb teaches embodiment. Nut teaches vastness. Geb says: you are made of matter. Nut says: you are open to the stars. Geb is the body kneeling in soil. Nut is the mind looking upward. Between them stands Shu, holding open the space where life may breathe.

With Asar, Aset, Set, and Nebet-Het, the Pesedjet moves from cosmic architecture into drama. Now creation becomes fertility, lineage, disruption, repair, death, hiddenness, boundary, grief, loyalty, betrayal, restoration, and moral consequence. Life regenerates. Love gathers. Disruption breaks. Boundary protects. Grief remembers. Repair begins.

But differentiation alone is not enough. A universe can differentiate into chaos. A society can differentiate into hierarchy. A mind can differentiate into fragmentation. A family can differentiate into estrangement. Therefore, the Pesedjet requires Ma'at. The Ogdoad gives potential. Atum/Ptah gives center and articulation. The Pesedjet gives structure. Ma'at gives right relationship.

Chapter 5 - Ma'at: Right Measure, Right Relation

The world does not become sacred because it exists. The world becomes sacred when relation is held in right measure. A body can exist and still be disordered. A family can exist and still be wounded. A civilization can exist and still be cruel. A universe can differentiate and still require coherence. This is why the Pesedjet is not enough.

Ma'at is one of the deepest words in the Nile Valley spiritual imagination: goddess, principle, law, measure, truth, order, justice, reciprocity, and cosmic balance. For SDAE, Ma'at is not treated as a physical force. It is not gravity, electromagnetism, dark energy, a hidden particle, or a new field. Ma'at is read as an ancestral symbolic name for right relationship.

Balance is often misunderstood. Many people hear balance and imagine equal halves: fifty percent here, fifty percent there. Living systems rarely survive by equal division. A body is not healthy because every chemical is present in equal quantity. A star is not stable because gravity and radiation pressure are equal in a shallow arithmetic way. A grieving person may need silence more than advice. A sick body may need rest more than activity. Balance does not mean 50/50. Balance means the right relationship for stability, dignity, and renewal.

SDAE distinguishes dormant Ma'at and kinetic Ma'at. In the Ogdoad, Ma'at is not yet law in motion. There are no stars to hold, no bodies to regulate, no societies to guide, no hearts to weigh. Yet if a world is to emerge at all, the possibility of right relation must already be latent. Ma'at sleeps in the Deep; Ma'at awakens when the world requires right relation.

The Ogdoad is not Isfet. The Ogdoad is pre-form potential. Isfet is active disorder after order has become possible. Ma'at is not the enemy of the Ogdoad. Ma'at is the organizer of emergence from the Ogdoad. Mystery is not the enemy. Violation is the enemy.

Ma'at can be described as qualitative geometry: the geometry of right relationship. A healthy body has geometry: cellular organization, tissue architecture, circulation, signaling, rhythms, and boundaries. A healthy family has geometry: elders, children, stories, responsibilities, limits, forgiveness, truth, and care. A healthy society has geometry: justice, distribution, memory, accountability, education, and protection.

In SDAE notation, Ma'at may be written symbolically as $M\_a = R(T, J, C, P, E)$, where T is truth, J justice, C coherence, P proportion, and E ethical reciprocity. This is not a field equation. It is a teaching equation. It says Ma'at is the relational state in which truth, justice, coherence, proportion, and reciprocity are held together.

Chapter 6 - Isfet and Set: Necessary Disruption versus Destructive Disorder

The Deep is not evil. Darkness is not evil. The unknown is not evil. Mystery is not evil. A storm is not always evil. An ending is not always evil. A boundary is not always evil. A disruption is not always evil. This is one of the most important lessons in Sacred Divine Spirituality.

If we confuse the primordial Deep with destruction, we become afraid of mystery. If we confuse disruption with evil, we become afraid of change. If we confuse Set with Isfet, we lose the ability to understand necessary force. And if we confuse Isfet with creative transformation, we begin excusing cruelty, domination, and fragmentation as though they were sacred.

The distinction is simple: the Ogdoad is primordial potential; Set is disruptive force within creation; Isfet is destructive disorder against coherence. The Ogdoad is the Deep before form. Set is the storm inside the world. Isfet is the violation of Ma'at.

Set is not identical with Isfet. Set is storm, desert, force, rupture, danger, and boundary-breaking. He is difficult and dangerous, but not the same as absolute uncreation. When governed by Ma'at, force can defend the boundary. When divorced from Ma'at, force becomes violence. Set under Ma'at protects. Set under Isfet destroys.

A seed must split for the plant to rise. A child must leave the womb. A family secret must sometimes be spoken. A sick body may need to purge, rest, sweat, cry, or break a harmful rhythm. A person may need to leave a destructive relationship. A civilization may need to abandon a false story about itself. These are disruptions, but they are not necessarily Isfet.

Isfet is falsehood, cruelty, humiliation, domination, injustice, and relational collapse. In the body, Isfet appears as chronic stress without repair, exhaustion without rest, and inflammation without regulation. In the family, it appears as silence, cruelty, abandonment, and inherited trauma that becomes normal. In society, it appears as exploitation, ecological destruction, spiritual manipulation, and refusal to protect the vulnerable.

A NuSpecian practice follows: when the storm arrives, ask four questions. Is this Ogdoad - a dark, unformed space where something new has not yet appeared? Is this Set - disruptive force that may need to be governed or redirected? Is this Isfet - active harm or violation? Where is Ma'at - what restores right measure here?

Chapter 7 - Heru: The Return of Coherence

There comes a point in every sacred story when the world has already been created, but creation is not yet whole. The Deep has opened, the Center has appeared, the World has differentiated, Ma'at has been named, Set has risen, and Isfet has wounded the field. Now the question is no longer how the world began. The question becomes: how does the world return to right relationship after it has been broken?

This is where Heru enters. Known widely as Horus, Heru is not forced into the Ogdoad and not reduced to a simplistic parallel with Jesus. He is the symbolic teaching of coherence restored after fragmentation. He is what happens when grief does not become despair, when anger does not become cruelty, when memory does not become bitterness, and when the wounded field learns to see again.

Heru is not the beginning of creation. Heru is the return of creation to right measure. The Ogdoad is potential before form. Heru is consciousness after fracture. The Ogdoad is the Deep before the world. Heru is the world learning to restore itself.

Heru is not merely a tenth name. He is not arithmetically added to the Ennead. He is ethically generated by the crisis of the Ennead. Asar is wounded continuity. Aset is sacred gathering. Set is disruptive force. Nebet-Het is grief at the threshold. Ma'at is right relation. Heru is the restored field.

The Eye of Heru is a symbol of restored perception after conflict. The eye sees. The wounded eye sees through pain. The restored eye sees through wisdom. The restored eye is not innocent; it is coherent. In Holofractal SDAE language, the part carries the wound of the whole, and the part also carries the possibility of whole-system return.

Heru is also forgiveness, but forgiveness must be defined carefully. Forgiveness is not denial, not returning to danger, not pretending harm did not happen, not spiritual performance. Forgiveness is the release of Isfet from ruling the Spirit Field. A person may forgive and still keep a boundary, tell the truth, refuse reconciliation, require justice, and grieve.

SDAE may write Heru as $H\_R = R(M\_a, W, B, G, S)$, where M_a is Ma'at, W wound, B boundary, G grief integrated rather than denied, and S restored sight. Heru is the restoration of Ma'at after wound, through boundary, grief, and restored sight.

Chapter 8 - African Sacred Measure: Memory, Mathematics, and Restoration Without Resentment

There is a kind of forgetting that wounds the future. A person can forget where they placed a tool. A family can forget an old story. A people can forget their ancestral language. A civilization can forget who first taught it to measure the sky, heal the body, align stone, organize time, and bind ethics to the order of the cosmos.

When memory is broken, the wound does not remain in the past. It enters the body, education, religion, science, and the way a people sees itself. This chapter is not written to replace one supremacy with another. It is written to restore Ma'at to memory.

The Nile Valley was not outside the history of mathematics. Kemet and Kush were not outside the history of science. African spiritual systems were not merely superstition. The Neteru were not merely fantasy figures. Ma'at was not merely morality. Sacred measure was not merely decoration. These were ways of organizing life, sky, body, ritual, ethics, architecture, and consciousness into one coherent field.

Djehuty - often called Thoth - represents more than writing. He is measure, record, reckoning, proportion, language, memory, and the disciplined intelligence that keeps the world from dissolving into confusion. To measure is not merely to count. To measure is to enter into relation with reality.

Greek geometry formalized; Nile Valley geometry functioned. Euclid's formalization matters, but it does not erase earlier functional geometry: land surveying, slope, area, volume, granaries, stone, calendar, and temple proportion. Ma'at restores them to right relation. There is no need to diminish later formal mathematics in order to honor earlier sacred measure.

African recursive and fractal design traditions also matter. A village can mirror the family. The family can mirror the lineage. The lineage can mirror the cosmos. The temple can mirror the body. The body can mirror the universe. The breath can mirror expansion and return. This is not decorative; it is pedagogical. The pattern teaches the law.

The African originality chapter must not become a war cry. The stronger message is this: the world is more truthful, more whole, and more coherent when African memory is restored to its rightful place. This is not anti-anyone. It is pro-Ma'at.

Chapter 9 - Djehuty, Mathematics, and the Language of the Cosmos

Before mathematics becomes equation, it is attention. Before attention becomes number, it is relation. Before relation becomes geometry, it is measure. And before measure becomes civilization, someone must remember. This is why Djehuty matters.

Mathematics is not only quantity. It is relation. A ratio is relation. A symmetry is relation. A sequence is relation. A boundary is relation. A transformation is relation. A pattern across scale is relation. A recurrence is relation. A proof is relation held without contradiction.

The Nile Valley was a civilization of measure. Flood, field, grain, stone, slope, temple, star, calendar, wound, medicine, offering, law, inheritance, burial, and memory all required measure. This is why Sacred Divine Spirituality is not asking people to admire vague mystery. It asks people to recover disciplined spiritual intelligence.

The seked is a beautiful example. A slope is not a thing by itself. A slope is a relationship: horizontal run to vertical rise, earth to sky, foundation to ascent. A pyramid cannot rise coherently if its slope lacks proportion. A life cannot rise coherently if its foundation lacks proportion. A society cannot rise coherently if its base is unjust.

The 3-4-5 triangle is another teaching image: $3^2 + 4^2 = 5^2$. A right triangle is not stable because its numbers are magical. It is stable because the sides are in lawful relation. Symbolically, Asar can be read as depth and ancestry, Aset as matrix and care, and Heru as the living resultant of memory and care. This is teaching geometry, not historical proof.

The Eye of Heru fraction series can be used carefully as symbolic teaching: $1/2 + 1/4 + 1/8 + 1/16 + 1/32 + 1/64 = 63/64$. The series shows a whole divided into smaller and smaller parts, approaching completion while leaving a remainder. It teaches that measurement approaches reality, but perspective never exhausts reality.

Fibonacci teaches unfolding through sequential memory. Phi teaches proportional convergence. Ma'at teaches right measure. The disciplined SDAE triad is: Fibonacci is growth through sequence; Phi is proportion approached through growth; Ma'at is right relationship that allows growth to remain life-giving.

Djehuty can be written symbolically as $D\_j = R(M, N, S, T, C)$, where M is measure, N number, S symbol, T truthful record across time, and C coherence. Knowledge becomes sacred when it serves Ma'at.

Chapter 10 - Holofractal SDAE: The Part Carries the Whole

A seed is not the forest, yet the forest is hidden in the seed. A cell is not the body, yet the body is encoded through the cell. A child is not the ancestor, yet the ancestor lives through the child. A temple is not the cosmos, yet a temple may be built so the cosmos can be remembered in stone. A human being is not the universe, yet the human body carries star-forged elements, planetary chemistry, ancestral memory, biological rhythm, emotional history, and the power of consciousness to look back upon the cosmos and ask what it means.

This is the first intuition of Holofractal SDAE: the part is not the whole, but the part may carry the trace of the whole. Holofractal does not mean that everything is literally the same thing. It means certain patterns of relation, recursion, boundary, coherence, fragmentation, restoration, and perspective may recur across scales.

The Ogdoad recurs wherever life enters the unformed Deep. A person waiting for test results stands in a small Ogdoad. A family grieving a loved one stands in a small Ogdoad. A scientist at the edge of quantum gravity stands in a mathematical Ogdoad. The Deep appears at every scale where form has not yet become clear.

Atum/Ptah recurs wherever a new center and articulation appear. A person in crisis needs a first center. The first center may be a breath, a truth, a diagnosis, a boundary, a prayer, a care plan, a meal, a night of sleep, or a decision not to become cruel.

The Pesedjet recurs wherever a system differentiates into parts. A body needs organs. A mind needs distinct capacities. A family needs roles. A society needs institutions. A science needs disciplines. But differentiation creates danger: parts can lose relation. Every differentiated system faces the same question: will the parts remain in right relation?

Ma'at is cross-scale coherence. At the biological scale, Ma'at is regulation, rhythm, repair, and nourishment. At the psychological scale, Ma'at is integration. At the family scale, Ma'at is truth and care. At the social scale, Ma'at is justice. At the spiritual scale, Ma'at is coherence between inner and outer life.

Heru is holofractal return. He appears wherever a field has been wounded and must return to coherence: a wounded eye, body, family, people, planet, memory, science, or religion. Heru teaches that restoration is not return to innocence. It is coherence after experience.

Sacred Divine Spirituality may be expressed symbolically as SDS = H(O, C, M_a, H_R, D_j, Psi). In plain language: Sacred Divine Spirituality is the holofractal practice of living from the Deep, finding center, holding right measure, restoring coherence after wound, recording truth, and organizing the inner field through meaning, value, compassion, and relation.

Chapter 11 - Cosmology Becomes Theology: Sacred Story as Teaching Technology

Before theology becomes doctrine, it is usually a story about the world. Before the priest explains law, someone has watched the sky. Before scripture becomes canon, someone has wondered why there is light, water, death, birth, storm, order, disorder, love, and fear.

Cosmology becomes theology when the structure of the world becomes a teaching about how to live. The stars become signs. The river becomes blessing. The storm becomes judgment. The sun becomes life. The deep becomes mystery. The heart becomes a scale. The sky becomes throne. The body becomes a temporary dwelling. The ancestor becomes memory. The child becomes continuation.

Sacred story is a teaching technology. It allows a people to remember cosmic order, moral order, social order, ecological order, and interior order before most people can read mathematics, philosophy, or medicine. A formula can describe a relation; a story can train a life.

The Neteru can be read as sacred personifications of powers, principles, relations, and forces of nature and consciousness. This does not mean the book demands that every reader worship them. It means the book invites readers to understand them as one ancient way of organizing reality.

The Bible did not fall into history without culture. It emerged in the ancient Near Eastern world, where creation, flood, covenant, law, kingship, exile, temple, sacrifice, judgment, restoration, and divine sovereignty were already meaningful teaching languages. Sacred traditions develop in places, languages, institutions, and cultures.

Contact does not mean collapse. Resonance does not mean replacement. Heru and Jesus can be compared structurally without being collapsed into each other. African, Jewish, Christian, Islamic, Greek, Roman, and later philosophical traditions all wrestle with the same great questions: What is the Source? How does order emerge? Why does suffering exist? How is coherence restored? What remains when the body returns?

Theology can comfort, and theology can wound. It comforts when it says: you are loved, not alone, and not reduced to your illness. It wounds when it says: you are sick because God is punishing you, or you are not healed because your faith is weak. Sacred Divine Spirituality refuses to let theology become Isfet.

Chapter 12 - Heru and Jesus: Structural Resonance, Not Copy-Paste

There are comparisons that illuminate and comparisons that distort. A shallow comparison collapses one tradition into another. A deeper comparison asks why human beings, across cultures and centuries, keep telling sacred stories about a wounded world, a restoring figure, a battle against disorder, and the return of right relationship.

Heru is not Jesus. Jesus is not Heru. They belong to different traditions, languages, histories, scriptures, and theological worlds. Heru belongs to the Nile Valley sacred drama of Asar, Aset, Set, Ma'at, kingship, order, and restoration. Jesus belongs to Jewish, early Christian, and later global Christian theology, with its doctrines of incarnation, redemption, resurrection, covenant, grace, and salvation.

Yet a structural resonance exists: the world is wounded, a restoring figure appears, disorder must be confronted, a sacrifice or wound is endured, sight, order, or life is restored, and the community is asked to live differently. This pattern matters because it helps us understand why cosmology becomes theology.

For Heru, the wound is the violation of Ma'at through Set's disruption and Asar's death. For Jesus, within Christian theology, the wound is sin, death, estrangement, suffering, and humanity's need for redemption. The traditions differ. The structure resonates. That is enough.

Heru restores Ma'at. Jesus, for Christians, restores relation to God. Heru answers Set's violation. Jesus answers sin, death, and estrangement. Heru belongs to the sacred order of Kemet and the drama of kingship, order, grief, and repair. Jesus belongs to Jewish and Christian sacred history: covenant, prophecy, kingdom, cross, resurrection, redemption, and new life.

The Eye of Heru and the cross of Jesus are not the same symbol. But both teach that restoration passes through wound. The eye can be wounded and still be restored. The cross can be carried and still become a doorway of meaning for Christians. Neither sacred system offers cheap triumph. Real restoration honors the wound without surrendering the future to it.

This chapter is not for religious debate alone. It is for people who are suffering. The sacred story does not always say, "No suffering will come." It says, "Suffering must not become the final meaning." When physical cure does not come, there may still be dignity, forgiveness, love, family, memory, and the chance to bless those who remain.

Chapter 13 - The One, the Deep, and the Word: Judaism, Christianity, Islam, and SDAE

There is a moment in every serious spiritual life when the question becomes simple and terrible: Where is God when the body suffers? Not in theory, but in the hospital room, in the silence after the diagnosis, in the long night of pain, in the prayer that did not seem to bring the cure.

This is where theology must become tender. A theology that cannot sit beside the sick has lost Ma'at. A theology that can explain heaven but cannot protect dignity on Earth has lost its way. A theology that blames the suffering for their suffering has become Isfet.

Judaism, Christianity, and Islam speak of God. SDAE speaks philosophically of a primordial undifferentiated root. These are not the same category. A theologian may speak of God as personal, sovereign, creator, merciful, judge, redeemer. SDAE speaks of one reality prior to differentiation into outer structure and inner experience. The bridge is not equivalence; the bridge is reverence.

Judaism gives the language of covenant, memory, law, and moral return. Christianity gives the language of incarnation, cross, resurrection, redemption, and embodied restoration. Islam gives the language of Tawhid, surrender, mercy, and return to the One. Kemet and Kush give the language of Neteru, Ogdoad, Pesedjet, Ma'at, Djehuty, Heru, and sacred measure. SDAE gives the language of one root, two aspects, outer structure, inner experience, consciousness at the threshold, and Spirit as structured interior coherence.

The Word matters because suffering becomes more terrifying when it cannot be named. A person says: I feel abandoned. I am afraid. I need help. I am angry at God. I do not want to die. I still love my family. I want to forgive. I am not ready. The Word begins restoration because it gives shape to the Deep.

A client says, "I prayed. Why am I still sick?" Do not argue. Do not say, "Everything happens for a reason," if it lands like cruelty. Begin with dignity. Say: I hear how painful that is. When the body suffers and the cure does not come, it can feel like God is silent. I do not want to take your faith away. I want to help you breathe inside this moment.

The physical cure and the cosmological cure are not the same. A physical cure means the disease is reversed, removed, stabilized, or successfully treated. A cosmological cure means the person's meaning, dignity, inner coherence, family love, spiritual orientation, and sense of belonging to life are restored even when the physical outcome is uncertain.

Chapter 14 - Sacred Divine Living: Body, Nature, Family, and Earth in Right Measure

A sacred life is not proven by what a person says about heaven. It is proven by how the person lives on Earth: how they treat the body, speak to the sick, feed the hungry, forgive without lying, rest without guilt, care for children and elders, honor nature, protect clean water and clean air, carry grief without becoming cruel, and practice faith without postponing compassion.

Sacred Divine Living is not escape. It is right relationship: Ma'at in the body, Ma'at in the family, Ma'at in the community, Ma'at in the Earth, Ma'at in the Spirit Field. This is where spirituality becomes practical.

The body is not an enemy. The body is not a punishment. The body is not merely a shell to be discarded. The body is a sovereign kingdom. It has rivers and gates, messengers and boundaries, fires and cooling systems, workers and repair crews, memory and rhythm, organs and laws.

Illness is not moral failure. Cancer is not proof of weak faith. Chronic disease is not proof of spiritual inferiority. A tired body is not a sinful body. A disabled body is not a failed body. An aging body is not an abandoned body. A dying body is not a punished body. Sacred Divine Spirituality must never blame the suffering. It must ask: where can Ma'at still be restored?

Metabolic peace is sacred. A stressed body becomes a loud body. A sleep-deprived body becomes reactive. An inflamed body becomes burdened. A dehydrated body becomes strained. A body under constant humiliation, fear, overwork, grief, or discrimination begins to carry pressure in its chemistry. Reduce the burden where you can: protect sleep, hydrate, move gently, eat truthfully, breathe slowly, seek help, and let the body repair.

Sacred Divine Living can be organized through twelve practices of right measure: metabolism and energy regulation; hormones and endocrine stress; immune and inflammatory signaling; mitochondria and oxidative balance; genomic stability and repair; tissue remodeling; purification and detox support; autophagy fasting when appropriate; stress management; spiritual coherence; meditation; and supplementing or rebuilding with appropriate professional guidance.

Coherence is not perfection. Coherence is return. A star is coherent not because nothing pulls on it, but because its forces remain in dynamic relation. A family is coherent not because no one ever disagrees, but because truth and love can eventually find each other again. A Spirit Field is coherent not because it is never wounded, but because meaning, value, compassion, and relation can reorganize after wound.

Chapter 15 - Lineage Resonance: Ancestors, Family Fields, and the Afterlife of Compassion

A body can die. A kindness can continue. A voice can grow quiet. A teaching can remain. A hand can release its final grip. A family can still feel the warmth that hand once gave. Human beings do not continue in only one way. Biology has its season. The body has its time. But life is also process.

Biological Life is the living body: breath, circulation, metabolism, digestion, repair, immune signaling, hormones, tissues, organs, nerves, and cellular energy. Process Life is the continuing pattern: memory, influence, story, virtue, teaching, family culture, social impact, moral example, and the love that remains active in those who were touched.

The body returns to nature. The breath returns to air. The minerals return to soil. The atoms continue in the great motion. The person's physical form ends, but the matter that carried that form re-enters the world. Do not hate the body because it is temporary. Honor the body because it carried you.

Lineage Resonance is the way a life continues to vibrate through family, community, memory, values, stories, habits, blessings, wounds, repairs, and acts of compassion after the biological body has completed its role. It is not a replacement for anyone's religious afterlife. It is a life-on-Earth teaching.

Every family is a field: memory, habits, stories, wounds, blessings, repeated phrases, inherited fears, familiar meals, old songs, quiet resentments, and sacred tenderness. A coherent family field tells the truth without destroying one another, remembers ancestors without idolizing them, allows grief without rushing it, and protects children from inherited Isfet.

Wounds travel too. A grandfather's humiliation can become a family's anger. A mother's unprocessed grief can become a daughter's anxiety. A father's silence can become a son's emotional absence. A people's erased history can become generations of lowered expectation. The purpose is not to worship the past. The purpose is to restore Ma'at to the lineage.

Lineage Resonance can be written symbolically as $L\_R = R(M, V, A, C, T)$: memory, virtue, ancestral influence, compassion transmitted, and truth carried forward. Biology returns to nature. Process enters the lineage field.

Chapter 16 - Sacred Death and the Cosmological Cure

There is a kind of healing that does not always cure the body. There is a kind of peace that does not require pretending death is far away. There is a kind of courage that does not deny fear. Sacred Divine Spirituality must speak here tenderly, because the sick person does not need another theory if the theory cannot become compassion.

A physical cure treats the disease. A cosmological cure restores the field of meaning around the person. A physical cure asks whether the illness can be reversed, removed, stabilized, or controlled. A cosmological cure asks whether the person can remain dignified, loved, coherent, truthful, remembered, forgiven, comforted, and held in right relationship while the body changes.

These are not the same. If a physical cure is possible, seek it. If treatment can help, honor it. If surgery, medication, nutrition, therapy, palliative care, hospice, counseling, prayer, family support, or clinical care is needed, let care be welcomed. Sacred Divine Spirituality does not reject help. It blesses honest help.

If the physical cure does not come, we must not say nothing remains. There is still breath, touch, truth, forgiveness where forgiveness is ready, family, memory, dignity, Ma'at, and the possibility of the heart becoming lighter before the final breath.

Death is not punishment. Aging is not punishment. Illness is not always punishment. A body changing form is not proof that God has withdrawn love. A dying body is not evidence that faith has failed. Nature is not evil because bodies are temporary. The body is sacred, but it is not permanent.

A sacred death is not necessarily painless or fearless. It is a death held in dignity: truth without cruelty, hope without deception, care without abandonment, silence without neglect, prayer without pressure, medicine without coldness, family without chaos, grief without shame, and forgiveness without force.

The four bedside questions are simple: What do you want us to remember? What do you want us to carry forward? What do you want released? What blessing do you want to give? These questions give the dying person authorship and give the family a way to become Heru by carrying forward what was good and releasing what should not continue.

Chapter 17 - The Honorable Challenges: Einstein, Penrose, and Smolin Question SDAE

A serious framework must welcome serious challengers. If a philosophy cannot survive questions, it is not yet philosophy. If a metaphysics cannot distinguish metaphor from mechanism, it becomes confusion. If a spirituality cannot honor science, it becomes fantasy. This chapter invites Einstein, Penrose, and Smolin into the room not as enemies, but as guardians of rigor.

Einstein asks: where are the equations? If you speak of fields, curvature, gravity, geometry, and spacetime, you must distinguish metaphor from physical law. SDAE answers: we do not claim to rewrite general relativity. We use curvature as disciplined metaphor for interior life, not as a replacement for spacetime physics. A grieving person's inner world may be curved by loss, but that is not Einsteinian spacetime curvature.

Einstein also warns: do not confuse awe with evidence. SDAE agrees. Awe is not evidence for physics, but awe is evidence that interior life is real. Any complete philosophy of reality must account for the fact that the universe produces beings capable of awe, compassion, grief, and moral responsibility.

Penrose asks: what do you mean by consciousness? Are you claiming consciousness is everywhere? Are particles conscious? Did the primordial condition already think? SDAE answers: no. Experiential potential may belong to the root, but actual consciousness emerges only where coherent, integrated, self-modeling structure crosses a threshold. Potential is not manifestation.

Penrose also challenges Holofractal SDAE: what is the mathematical object? Graph, tensor network, category, spin network, simplicial complex? SDAE answers: we do not yet know. The equations are symbolic scaffolding for future theory work. They are not completed physics.

Smolin asks: can this be tested? Does SDAE make physical predictions? Does it explain dark matter, dark energy, consciousness, or cosmological evolution? SDAE answers honestly: at present, SDAE is not a competing cosmological model. It does not replace ΛCDM, identify dark matter, solve the cosmological constant problem, or experimentally detect the Spirit Field. It is a metaphysical framework that may inspire future testable models, but must not pretend to already be one.

The honorable challenge protects SDAE from becoming a false theory of everything. SDAE is not a completed theory of everything. It is a disciplined metaphysical framework for interpreting one reality through two irreducible modes: outer structure and inner experience. Its equations are symbolic scaffolds. Its Spirit Field is structured interior coherence, not a physical force. Its spirituality is life-on-Earth coherence, not a replacement for anyone's religion.

33

Chapter 18 - The Universe Is Inexhaustibly Knowable

The human mind wants a final equation: one line, one law, one master key, one door through which all mystery becomes solved. But the universe behaves more like a living scroll: every age reads one layer, then finds another hidden beneath it. No single language has exhausted reality.

Before mathematics becomes equation, it is relation. Before relation becomes geometry, it is possibility. Before possibility becomes law, it is dormant coherence. This is the idea of Dormant Mathematical Potential. The primordial condition did not contain all equations as finished human symbols. It contained the potential for lawful relation, and therefore the dormant possibility of future mathematics.

The Law of Dormant Mathematical Potential may be stated this way: all mathematics exists first as latent relational possibility within the primordial undifferentiated condition. As reality differentiates into stable regimes of structure, boundary, recursion, and perspective, corresponding mathematical languages become possible. Human mathematics is therefore not the possession of reality's total form, but the progressive disclosure of patterns consciousness becomes capable of recognizing.

Humanity did not always have calculus, non-Euclidean geometry, tensor calculus, quantum mechanics, topology, category theory, information geometry, chaos theory, fractal geometry, or network theory. These languages appeared because human beings encountered aspects of reality older languages could not contain. New realities call forth new mathematics.

The universe may disclose mathematics by regime. Pre-geometric regimes may require one kind of thought; geometrogenesis another; vacuum and inflation another; fields and particles another; stars another; chemistry another; life another; consciousness another; ethics another; Spirit Field coherence another. SDAE does not say these are all the same mathematics. It says each regime calls forth the mathematics adequate to its relational structure.

The universe is not unknowable in a hopeless sense. It is inexhaustibly knowable. We can know more, but may never know all. We can discover laws, but may never possess the whole law. We can build mathematics, but may need future mathematics beyond present imagination.

Ma'at is the ethics of knowing. Know truthfully. Know humbly. Know proportionately. Know without domination. Know without erasing the human being. Know without claiming finality too soon. Knowledge without Ma'at becomes Isfet.

Conclusion - Sacred Divine Spirituality: The Return to Ma'at

At the end of this journey, we return to a simple truth: the human being must live in right relationship. Not merely believe correctly, think deeply, pray beautifully, measure accurately, speak of the universe, honor ancestors, or admire the stars. Live in right relationship - with the body, nature, family, science, faith, memory, grief, the dying, the living, the Earth, and the hidden mystery from which all forms arise.

This is Sacred Divine Spirituality. It is not a new religion competing with ancient ones. It is not a doctrine demanding that Christians cease being Christian, Muslims cease being Muslim, Jews cease being Jewish, African traditionalists cease honoring ancestors, or scientists cease honoring evidence. It is a way of living on Earth.

Sacred does not mean escaping nature. Sacred means honoring what carries life: river, soil, body, family, elder, child, sick person, dying person, Earth, cosmos. Divine does not mean detached from the world. Divine means participating in the deepest order of reality: breath, nourishment, sleep, apology, forgiveness, boundary, clean water, honest medicine, family tenderness, and the refusal to call cruelty holy.

Spirituality is coherent resonance between inner and outer life, cultivated through rhythm, nourishment, movement, stillness, truth, relation, and reciprocity with the living world. This sentence is the bridge. It does not require abandoning science or faith. It simply says the inner life and outer life must be brought into right relationship.

The NuSpecian sacred form remains: We come from the cosmos. We are sustained by nature. We become whole through balance. Therefore let body, mind, relation, and Earth be kept in right measure.

One of the central ethical teachings of this book is that illness must not become shame. A sick body is not a failed body. A dying body is not a punished body. A disabled body is not a spiritually inferior body. The NuSpecian health regime is support, not blame: a coherence practice for the sovereign kingdom of the body.

A physical cure treats the disease. A cosmological cure restores meaning, dignity, love, forgiveness, family coherence, lineage resonance, and Spirit Field coherence when the body's outcome is uncertain or final. If the physical cure comes, receive it with gratitude. If it does not come, do not say nothing remains.

The dying person is not being erased. The body returns. The process continues. The atoms return to nature. The breath returns to air. The love enters memory. The virtues enter lineage. The kindness becomes ancestral gravity. The story travels. The family field carries what was good.

African memory must be restored without bitterness. Kemet, Kush, Ta-Seti, Khmunu, Iunu, the Ogdoad, Pesedjet, Ma'at, Heru, Djehuty, Aset, Asar, Set, Nebet-Het, Amun, Ptah, and Atum do not need resentment. They need accuracy, reverence, study, and descendants who can carry forward wisdom without becoming trapped in grievance.

SDAE's boundary is its strength. SDAE is not a completed theory of everything, not new physics, not a new force, not a medical cure, not proof that consciousness controls matter, and not a replacement for religion or medicine. It is a disciplined metaphysical framework: one root, two irreducible aspects, correlated emergence, consciousness at the threshold, Spirit as structured interior coherence.

Sacred Divine Spirituality can now be stated as a doctrine of living: Sacred Divine Spirituality is the practice of living in coherent resonance with body, nature, family, Earth, science, ancestry, mystery, and the Divine Cosmos, so that inner experience and outer structure are held in Ma'at. Or more simply: Sacred Divine Spirituality is Ma'at made daily.

Do not merely believe in Ma'at. Live Ma'at. Do not merely speak of Heru. Return like Heru. Do not merely name Djehuty. Write truth like Djehuty. Do not merely honor ancestors. Become an ancestor worth remembering. Do not merely say the body is sacred. Care for the body. Do not merely say Earth is sacred. Protect Earth. Do not merely say love is eternal. Practice love while breath remains.

Appendix A - NuSpecian Covenant

I will honor the body because it carries consciousness. I will honor nature because nature sustains the body. I will honor science because truth must be measured where measurement is possible. I will honor spirituality because meaning must be lived where measurement ends. I will honor faith without using faith to blame the sick. I will honor medicine without letting medicine erase dignity.

I will honor ancestors without becoming trapped in resentment. I will honor grief without rushing the grieving. I will honor forgiveness without forcing denial. I will honor boundaries without becoming cruel. I will honor love by practicing it before it becomes memory. I will honor Ma'at by restoring right relation where my life touches the world.

This covenant is not perfection. It is return. Not domination. Coherence. Not fear. Ma'at.

Appendix B - Key Terms and Restored Names

Amun/Amaunet - Hiddenness, concealment, and the unseen principle of the Ogdoad.

Asar/Wesir (Osiris) - Ancestral continuity, fertility, death, regeneration, and the seed hidden in transformation.

Aset/Auset (Isis) - Gathering care, devotion, healing intelligence, and the power to restore what was scattered.

Atum - The first center, self-arising emergence, and the symbolic point from which ordered relation begins.

Djehuty/Tehuti (Thoth) - Measure, writing, number, record, truthful memory, and disciplined sacred intelligence.

Geb - Earth, embodiment, ground, matter, and the weight-bearing foundation of life.

Heru (Horus) - Restored sight, rightful return, conscious stewardship, and coherence after fragmentation.

Isfet - Active destructive disorder, falsehood, injustice, violation, and relational collapse after order has become possible.

Kemet - Ancient Egypt, especially as restored in this work as an African/Nile Valley civilization of sacred measure.

Khmunu/Khemenu - The City of the Eight, associated with the Ogdoad.

Kush / Ta-Seti / Nubia - Southern Nile Valley civilizations and source-regions central to African sacred memory.

Ma'at - Truth, justice, right measure, reciprocity, balance, order, and coherence as right relationship.

Nebet-Het (Nephthys) - Threshold, grief, hidden boundary, mourning, and liminal protection.

Nut - Sky, celestial vastness, star-bearing expanse, and the cosmic canopy.

Ogdoad - The Eightfold Deep: four primordial pairs of water, infinity, darkness, and hiddenness.

Pesedjet / Ennead - The Ninefold emergence of differentiated order in the Heliopolitan/Iunu tradition.

Ptah - The creative articulation of form: heart, speech, design, and the world becoming intelligible.

SDAE - Singularity Dual-Aspect Emergence: one root, two irreducible aspects, correlated emergence, consciousness at the threshold, Spirit as structured interior coherence.

Set - Storm, desert, force, rupture, necessary disruption when governed by Ma'at, destructive violence when captured by Isfet.

Shu - Breath, space, atmosphere, separation, and the room life needs to exist.

Spirit Field - The structured interior coherence of conscious life: meaning, value, compassion, integration, and relation. Not a physical field or force.

Tefnut - Moisture, binding, relational continuity, and life-bearing cohesion.

Appendix C - Before, During, and After Akhenaten: Spirituality, Ma'at, Atenism, and the Modern Cost of Separation

Statement of Scope

This appendix is interpretive, not accusatory. It does not argue that Akhenaten caused all later religious separation. It does not claim that Judaism, Christianity, or Islam are merely copied Egyptian religion. It does not blame monotheism for humanity's spiritual problems. It also does not romanticize pre-Akhenaten Kemet, Kush, Ta-Seti, or the Nile Valley as perfect societies free of hierarchy, war, priestly politics, or ordinary human suffering.

The purpose is more disciplined: to examine Akhenaten's religious revolution as a symbolic turning point in the history of spirituality - from distributed, nature-embedded sacred powers toward centralized, top-down divine mediation - and to ask what this shift means for Sacred Divine Spirituality today.

In SDAE language, this appendix asks: what happens when the many living laws of nature are collapsed into one distant source, mediated through power? And just as importantly: how can modern human beings recover the One without losing the many?

1. Before Akhenaten: Spirituality as a Field of Living Powers

Before Akhenaten, the spirituality of Kemet, Kush, Ta-Seti, and the broader Nile Valley world was not simply polytheism in the shallow sense of many competing gods. It was a symbolic ecology of powers, principles, places, forces, ancestors, rituals, bodies, temples, stars, rivers, and moral duties.

The Neteru were not merely supernatural personalities. They were also teaching powers: names for forces and principles through which nature, society, body, and cosmos could be interpreted. In this reading, the Neteru functioned as a sacred library of living powers - not modern physics, not modern chemistry, but an ancestral grammar of nature, order, healing, writing, measurement, fertility, boundary, kingship, grief, and restoration.

The Nile was sacred because it sustained agriculture. The sky was sacred because it ordered time. The heart was sacred because it carried moral weight. The body was sacred because it housed breath, vitality, memory, and consciousness. The king was sacred only insofar as he upheld Ma'at.

This is the crucial point: divine kingship before Akhenaten was ideally stewardship under Ma'at. The king did not create Ma'at. The king was answerable to Ma'at. He was supposed to maintain cosmic balance, temple order, justice, fertility, and continuity. In SDAE language, the king's legitimacy depended on whether he served coherence.

This older system was not perfect. It remained royal, hierarchical, and political. But spiritually it preserved a powerful truth: the divine was not encountered only outside the world; the divine was encountered through the world.

That is the part Sacred Divine Spirituality seeks to restore.

2. The Neteru as a Periodic Table of Sacred Nature

Modern chemistry uses symbols such as H, O, C, Fe, and Ca to name invisible principles of matter. Modern physics uses gravity, field, charge, spin, entropy, symmetry, and curvature to speak of invisible relations whose effects are visible.

The Nile Valley used sacred names such as Ma'at, Djehuty, Heru, Aset, Asar, Set, Sekhmet, Hapy, Ptah, Atum, Amun, Nut, Geb, Shu, and Tefnut to teach invisible powers of nature and life.

This does not mean the Neteru were modern chemistry or modern physics. It means they functioned as an ancestral teaching language.

Djehuty teaches measurement, writing, vibration, record, and disciplined intelligence. Sekhmet teaches heat, immune fire, danger, and transformative power. Hapy teaches river provision and agricultural dependence. Ptah teaches articulation, craftsmanship, and form. Heru teaches restoration of order after fragmentation. Ma'at teaches right relationship itself.

To honor Hapy was to understand dependence on the Nile. To honor Djehuty was to study measure and record. To honor Sekhmet was to respect fire, heat, danger, and healing. To honor Ma'at was to keep the heart, the state, and the cosmos in right relation.

Sacred Divine Spirituality can summarize this carefully: the Neteru gave humanity a sacred map of living powers.

3. During Akhenaten: The Aten and the Compression of the Sacred Field

Akhenaten's revolution was not a small reform. It was a radical compression of religious and political power. He elevated the Aten - the visible sun disk and life-giving radiance of sunlight - to the center of state religion. He changed his own name, moved the capital to Akhetaten, and reorganized the symbolic world around Aten devotion and royal mediation.

From an SDAE perspective, the Aten itself was not the problem. The sun is sacred. Light is sacred. Photosynthesis is sacred. Circadian rhythm is sacred. Solar energy is foundational to life. The body literally depends on the sun's gifts through food chains, climate, rhythm, and biological signaling.

The problem was compression.

Akhenaten did not simply teach that the sun is sacred. He compressed the sacred field into one state-centered channel. A rich ecology of Neteru - river, sky, measure, healing, storm, grief, fertility, death, restoration - was narrowed into a royal solar focus.

In SDAE language: the field of many living powers was compressed into one mediated source.

That is the Akhenaten break.

Not unity itself. Not sunlight itself. Not the One itself. The break was the loss of distributed sacred access.

4. What Was Gained

We should be fair.

Akhenaten's revolution may have intensified certain spiritual insights. It gave extraordinary focus to light. It emphasized the visible world and the life-giving power of the sun. It produced a striking artistic and devotional period. It may have sharpened the intuition that beneath many powers there is a unifying source.

So this appendix should not portray Akhenaten as simply wrong.

Atenism may be read as an early, dramatic attempt to say: behind the many powers, there is one radiant source.

SDAE can honor that. SDAE itself says: one root, two aspects, many expressions.

The insight of unity is not rejected. The question is whether unity remains in Ma'at.

5. What Was Lost

What appears to have been lost was the older distributed sacred ecology.

When the many Neteru are suppressed or flattened, the human being loses a nuanced map of nature. Instead of learning the many powers of the world - river, sky, measure, healing, fire, storm, fertility, death, grief, restoration - the people are directed toward one royal-sanctioned solar focus.

This is the core modern implication.

A spirituality detached from nature can become a spirituality detached from body. A spirituality detached from body can blame illness. A spirituality detached from Earth can exploit nature. A spirituality detached from Ma'at can defer compassion to the next life. A spirituality mediated through power can become domination.

This is why Sacred Divine Spirituality insists: do not defer Ma'at.

6. After Akhenaten: Restoration and Memory

Akhenaten's religious revolution did not endure in its original form. After his reign, Egypt moved back toward traditional religion. The older gods, temples, priesthoods, and ritual patterns returned in revised form.

But history rarely returns exactly to what it was.

The reaction after Akhenaten may have restored older public religious life, but it also preserved the memory of a difficult question: how can the One and the many belong together? How can unity be honored without erasing the living powers of nature? How can the hidden source be revered without turning the world into a spiritually secondary place?

That is exactly where SDAE enters.

7. The SDAE Interpretation: One Root, Many Living Powers

SDAE can read the Akhenaten crisis as a warning:

Unity without plurality can become spiritual monopoly. Plurality without unity can become fragmentation. The task is one root, many living powers, held in Ma'at.

Before Akhenaten, the sacred field preserved many powers. During Akhenaten, the sacred field was compressed into Aten and kingship. After Akhenaten, the older field returned, but the question of unity remained.

SDAE's answer is neither simple polytheism nor detached monotheism. SDAE says:

One root. Two aspects. Many expressions. One ethical demand: Ma'at.

The One must not erase the many. The many must not forget the One. The body must not be separated from spirit. Nature must not be separated from God. Science must not be separated from awe. Religion must not be separated from compassion. The afterlife must not be used to neglect life on Earth.

8. Could Things Have Been Better?

Yes - if unity had been integrated without suppression.

If Akhenaten had treated the Aten as the visible sign of a deeper unity while preserving the Neteru as living principles of nature, the revolution might have produced a more coherent synthesis:

Aten as light. Amun as hiddenness. Ptah as form. Djehuty as measure. Ma'at as order. Heru as restoration. Aset as gathering care. Asar as continuity through death. Sekhmet as fire and healing. Hapy as river provision.

That would have been closer to SDAE: one source, many expressions, no forced collapse of the sacred ecology.

If unity had not become royal monopoly, it might have deepened spiritual life rather than narrowing it. If the Aten had been taught as the solar face of Ma'at rather than the exclusive channel of divine power through Akhenaten, the reform might have become integration rather than rupture.

A better outcome might have been monotheistic depth without ecological separation; solar unity without suppression of nature's many laws; kingship under Ma'at rather than kingship over Ma'at.

9. Could Things Have Been Worse?

Yes - and in some ways the danger still lives today.

If the divine becomes distant, abstract, and mediated through authority, spirituality can become fear-based. If religious systems teach people to wait for another world while neglecting compassion in this one, Ma'at is weakened. If illness is interpreted as punishment, the sick person becomes spiritually wounded on top of bodily suffering.

This is not an attack on Judaism, Christianity, Islam, or monotheism. It is a warning to all religion: do not detach the One from the living world.

The One must become compassion. The One must become justice. The One must become care for the sick. The One must become clean water. The One must become ecological responsibility. The One must become truthful medicine. The One must become dignity before death.

A God who is only believed in, but not lived through compassion, has been separated from Ma'at.

10. Implications for Today

The modern world does not need to choose between Akhenaten and the old temple world. It needs a higher synthesis.

The lesson is not to return to the past exactly. The lesson is to restore what the past still knows that the present has forgotten.

The modern task is to recover sacred immanence without losing universal unity. We need the One, but we also need the many living laws of nature. We need God, but we also need body, breath, food, medicine, ecology, family, grief, and compassion. We need science, but we also need meaning. We need spirituality, but we also need Ma'at. We need religion, but we must not defer dignity to the next life.

This is why NuSpecian Sacred Divine Spirituality speaks to life on Earth:

We come from the cosmos. We are sustained by nature. We become whole through balance. Therefore let body, mind, relation, and Earth be kept in right measure.

11. Akhenaten as Warning and Teacher

Akhenaten should not be treated only as villain. He is also a teacher.

He teaches the power of unity. He teaches the danger of spiritual monopoly. He teaches that light can be sacred. He teaches that religious reform can become political control. He teaches that the visible world can inspire devotion. He teaches that devotion can become centralized authority. He teaches that the One must never be used to erase the many.

So the SDAE conclusion is:

Akhenaten saw light, but may have narrowed the field. The older Neteru preserved the field, but still required unity. SDAE restores both: the One and the many, the inner and the outer, science and spirit, body and cosmos, Ma'at and compassion.

12. Final Teaching

Before Akhenaten, spirituality was a field of living powers. During Akhenaten, spirituality became compressed through Aten and royal mediation. After Akhenaten, Egypt restored the older sacred ecology, but the memory of unity remained.

Today, humanity must not repeat the mistake of separation.

Do not separate God from nature. Do not separate spirit from body. Do not separate science from reverence. Do not separate medicine from dignity. Do not separate worship from compassion. Do not separate the afterlife from the life that is still being lived.

The sacred task is not to destroy monotheism, polytheism, science, or tradition. The sacred task is to restore Ma'at among them.

The One must breathe through the many. The many must remember the One. The body must be honored as nature. The Earth must be honored as sanctuary. The sick must not be blamed. The dying must not be abandoned. The living must not defer compassion.

That is the implication of Akhenaten for today.

That is the NuSpecian restoration.

That is Sacred Divine Spirituality.

Selected Bibliography and Source Traditions

Bibliographic Note: This bibliography gathers historical, scientific, philosophical, theological, and practice-oriented sources that informed the framework of this book. The ancient sources and modern scholarship support historical and conceptual background. The SDAE interpretations - including the Ogdoad-to-Ma'at-to-Heru sequence, Holofractal SDAE, Sacred Divine Spirituality, Lineage Resonance, and the Cosmological Cure - are the author's original metaphysical synthesis. These sources do not prove SDAE as physics; they provide the scholarly, scientific, and spiritual conversation within which SDAE is offered.

Allen, James P. Genesis in Egypt: The Philosophy of Ancient Egyptian Creation Accounts. Yale Egyptological Studies 2. New Haven: Yale Egyptological Seminar, 1988.

Allen, James P. The Ancient Egyptian Pyramid Texts. Atlanta: Society of Biblical Literature, 2005.

Aldred, Cyril. Akhenaten, King of Egypt. London: Thames & Hudson, 1988.

Assmann, Jan. The Search for God in Ancient Egypt. Translated by David Lorton. Ithaca: Cornell University Press, 2001.

Assmann, Jan. Moses the Egyptian: The Memory of Egypt in Western Monotheism. Cambridge, MA: Harvard University Press, 1997.

Bekenstein, Jacob D. "Black Holes and Entropy." Physical Review D 7, no. 8 (1973): 2333-2346.

Bohm, David. Wholeness and the Implicate Order. London: Routledge, 1980.

Breasted, James Henry. The Edwin Smith Surgical Papyrus. 2 vols. Chicago: University of Chicago Press, 1930.

Byock, Ira. Dying Well: Peace and Possibilities at the End of Life. New York: Riverhead, 1997.

Cassell, Eric J. "The Nature of Suffering and the Goals of Medicine." New England Journal of Medicine 306, no. 11 (1982): 639-645.

Chalmers, David J. The Conscious Mind: In Search of a Fundamental Theory. New York: Oxford University Press, 1996.

Chochinov, Harvey Max. Dignity Therapy: Final Words for Final Days. Oxford: Oxford University Press, 2012.

Clagett, Marshall. Ancient Egyptian Science: A Source Book. 3 vols. Philadelphia: American Philosophical Society, 1989-1999.

Damasio, Antonio. Self Comes to Mind: Constructing the Conscious Brain. New York: Pantheon, 2010.

Dodson, Aidan. Amarna Sunset: Nefertiti, Tutankhamun, Ay, Horemheb, and the Egyptian Counter-Reformation. Cairo: American University in Cairo Press, 2009.

Eglash, Ron. African Fractals: Modern Computing and Indigenous Design. New Brunswick, NJ: Rutgers University Press, 1999.

Emberling, Geoff, and Bruce Williams, eds. The Oxford Handbook of Ancient Nubia. Oxford: Oxford University Press, 2020.

Faulkner, Raymond O., trans. The Ancient Egyptian Coffin Texts. 3 vols. Warminster: Aris & Phillips, 1973-1978.

Frankl, Viktor E. Man's Search for Meaning. Boston: Beacon Press, 1959.

Gerdes, Paulus. Geometry from Africa: Mathematical and Educational Explorations. Washington, DC: Mathematical Association of America, 1999.

Gillings, Richard J. Mathematics in the Time of the Pharaohs. Cambridge, MA: MIT Press, 1972. Reprint, New York: Dover, 1982.

Hawking, Stephen W. "Particle Creation by Black Holes." Communications in Mathematical Physics 43 (1975): 199-220.

Hornung, Erik. Conceptions of God in Ancient Egypt: The One and the Many. Translated by John Baines. Ithaca: Cornell University Press, 1982.

James, William. The Varieties of Religious Experience. New York: Longmans, Green, 1902.

Kemp, Barry. The City of Akhenaten and Nefertiti: Amarna and Its People. London: Thames & Hudson, 2012.

Levenson, Jon D. Creation and the Persistence of Evil: The Jewish Drama of Divine Omnipotence. Princeton: Princeton University Press, 1988.

Lichtheim, Miriam. Ancient Egyptian Literature. 3 vols. Berkeley: University of California Press, 1973-1980.

Maldacena, Juan. "The Large N Limit of Superconformal Field Theories and Supergravity." Advances in Theoretical and Mathematical Physics 2 (1998): 231-252.

Murnane, William J. Texts from the Amarna Period in Egypt. Atlanta: Scholars Press, 1995.

Nagel, Thomas. "What Is It Like to Be a Bat?" The Philosophical Review 83, no. 4 (1974): 435-450.

Neugebauer, Otto, and Richard A. Parker. Egyptian Astronomical Texts. 3 vols. Providence: Brown University Press, 1960-1969.

Noether, Emmy. "Invariante Variationsprobleme." Nachrichten von der Gesellschaft der Wissenschaften zu Göttingen (1918): 235-257.

Nunn, John F. Ancient Egyptian Medicine. Norman: University of Oklahoma Press, 1996.

Penrose, Roger. The Road to Reality: A Complete Guide to the Laws of the Universe. New York: Alfred A. Knopf, 2004.

Penrose, Roger. Cycles of Time: An Extraordinary New View of the Universe. London: Bodley Head, 2010.

Pinch, Geraldine. Egyptian Mythology: A Guide to the Gods, Goddesses, and Traditions of Ancient Egypt. Oxford: Oxford University Press, 2002.

Planck Collaboration. "Planck 2018 Results. VI. Cosmological Parameters." Astronomy & Astrophysics 641 (2020): A6.

Quirke, Stephen. Ancient Egyptian Religion. London: British Museum Press, 1992.

Redford, Donald B. Akhenaten: The Heretic King. Princeton: Princeton University Press, 1984.

Riess, Adam G., et al. "Observational Evidence from Supernovae for an Accelerating Universe and a Cosmological Constant." Astronomical Journal 116 (1998): 1009-1038.

Robins, Gay, and Charles Shute. The Rhind Mathematical Papyrus: An Ancient Egyptian Text. London: British Museum Publications, 1987.

Rovelli, Carlo. Quantum Gravity. Cambridge: Cambridge University Press, 2004.

Rovelli, Carlo, and Francesca Vidotto. Covariant Loop Quantum Gravity. Cambridge: Cambridge University Press, 2014.

Rubin, Vera C., and W. Kent Ford Jr. "Rotation of the Andromeda Nebula from a Spectroscopic Survey of Emission Regions." Astrophysical Journal 159 (1970): 379-403.

Smolin, Lee. The Life of the Cosmos. New York: Oxford University Press, 1997.

Smolin, Lee. Time Reborn: From the Crisis in Physics to the Future of the Universe. Boston: Houghton Mifflin Harcourt, 2013.

Sulmasy, Daniel P. "A Biopsychosocial-Spiritual Model for the Care of Patients at the End of Life." The Gerontologist 42, suppl. 3 (2002): 24-33.

Susskind, Leonard. "The World as a Hologram." Journal of Mathematical Physics 36, no. 11 (1995): 6377-6396.

Tegmark, Max. Our Mathematical Universe. New York: Alfred A. Knopf, 2014.

Török, László. The Kingdom of Kush: Handbook of the Napatan-Meroitic Civilization. Leiden: Brill, 1997.

Varela, Francisco J., Evan Thompson, and Eleanor Rosch. The Embodied Mind: Cognitive Science and Human Experience. Cambridge, MA: MIT Press, 1991.

Weinberg, Steven. "The Cosmological Constant Problem." Reviews of Modern Physics 61 (1989): 1-23.

Whitehead, Alfred North. Process and Reality. New York: Macmillan, 1929.

Wilkinson, Richard H. The Complete Gods and Goddesses of Ancient Egypt. London: Thames & Hudson, 2003.

World Health Organization. Palliative Care. Fact sheets and clinical guidance.

Closing Bibliographic Note: The sources above do not close the question. They open it responsibly. Sacred Divine Spirituality is offered as an original SDAE synthesis - a disciplined bridge between African sacred memory, modern scientific humility, mathematical imagination, spiritual care, and the human need to live and die in Ma'at.

About the Author

Aston Farquharson is the founder of NuSpecies Integrative Practice, NuSpecies Press, and the originator of Singularity Dual-Aspect Emergence (SDAE), a NuSpecian philosophical framework exploring cosmology, consciousness, coherence, health, dignity, and human becoming.

His work seeks a disciplined bridge between science-respecting metaphysics, integrative wellness, ancestral restoration, environmental responsibility, and the interior questions that remain irreducible to physics alone. Through NuSpecies, he has developed Raw Organic Whole Foods formulas and educational frameworks intended to support body, mind, spirit, and life in right relationship with nature.

Farquharson is also an inventor and innovator with patents in physics and technologies granted worldwide, including work in renewable-energy concepts and prototype machines. His writing brings together scientific curiosity, philosophical reflection, ancestral memory, practical care, and a lifelong concern for health, healing, dignity, and the planet.